The Story of the Frisbee

By Alan Trussell-Cullen

Illustrated by Jon Davis

ᛒ Dominie Press, Inc.

Publisher: Raymond Yuen
Project Editor: John S. F. Graham
Editor: Bob Rowland
Designer: Greg DiGenti
Illustrator: Jon Davis

Published by:

℗ Dominie Press, Inc.

1949 Kellogg Avenue
Carlsbad, California 92008 USA

www.dominie.com

1-800-232-4570

Paperback ISBN 0-7685-1838-5
Printed in Singapore by PH Productions Pte Ltd
1 2 3 4 5 6 PH 05 04 03

Table of Contents

Chapter One
Pie in the Sky

Sometimes, inventions have very strange beginnings. In 1871, shortly after the Civil War, William Russell Frisbie moved to Bridgeport, Connecticut to manage a new bakery. William Frisbie liked his work so much that he decided to buy the bakery. He renamed it the Frisbie Pie Company.

The pies sold well—especially to students at the nearby colleges. One of those colleges was Yale. The college students not only liked to eat their Frisbie pies, but, so the story goes, they also liked sending the pie tins soaring through the air when they had finished eating!

The only problem was, if you happened to be passing by at the time, you were likely to be hit by one of those flying pie tins. They were made of metal and could be very painful on impact! So the students started yelling, "Frisbie!" just before they threw one, in order to warn any unsuspecting passersby.

Of course, like all good stories, there are different versions of this one. Another account of this story says it wasn't the

pie tins, but the lids to the Frisbie Pie Company's *cookie* tins. Another version is set over fifty years earlier and has a different man named Frisbie tossing a collection plate in church.

Whatever the real story is, the name *Frisbie* somehow came to mean that a flying, spinning disk was somewhere nearby.

Chapter Two
The Flying Saucers Are Coming

Fast-forward about seventy years.

Fred Morrison liked to throw things. During World War II he'd been a prisoner of war in one of the worst prison camps, so no wonder he wanted to throw things!

But like his father, he also had an

inventor's mind. (His father had invented a type of headlight for cars called "sealed beam." All cars today have sealed-beam headlights, so it was a very important invention!)

As a child, Morrison had thrown things like tin lids and metal disks and enjoyed watching them hover and float through the air. This was also a time when UFOs—unidentified flying objects—were capturing the country's imagination.

Morrison thought it would be a good time to market a toy that worked like a flying saucer. He tried making the toys out of metal, but they didn't act much like the flying saucers in the movies. So he tried making them out of plastic. He experimented with different shapes, and in 1951, he came up with what he

called the *Pluto Platter*.

One of the special features that helped it sail and hover extremely well was its curved edge, what is now called the "Morrison slope." This curved edge, unlike the pie tin's thin edge, made it easier to throw, kept it steady in the air, and made it fly farther.

It also had portholes on it—because everyone thought flying saucers had portholes so the visiting aliens could view the scenery as they flew over planet Earth!

The Pluto Platter sold reasonably well, but it wasn't a huge hit. Then Rich Knerr and A. K. "Spud" Melin came along and transformed the American skies.

Chapter Three

Wham-O
Comes Along

Rich Knerr and Spud Melin had their own toy company, Wham-O. They were responsible for some very famous toys, like the Hula-Hoop and the Super Ball.

The Hula-Hoop was a huge success in the 1950s. It seemed like almost everyone

was trying to wiggle a Hula-Hoop
around their hips.

The Super Ball was a hit, too. It was
made out of very condensed rubber,
so that when it bounced, it didn't just
bounce like an ordinary rubber ball,
it *really bounced*!

Rich and Spud were always on the
lookout for new toy ideas. In 1955, they
saw Morrison's Pluto Platter. They liked
what they saw. They managed to talk
Morrison into letting them sell his
invention, and a million dollars or so
later, he was probably glad he did!

Chapter Four
What's in a Name?

The Wham-O people thought that young people would most likely buy and throw Pluto Platters around. So they sent salespeople to high schools and universities around the United States.

At one of these universities, some

former students from Yale came along to watch the demonstrations.

"You know," they said to Rich Knerr, "years ago, students used to toss pie tins around like that. We called them *Frisbies* —after the company that made the pies."

"Is that right?" said Rich Knerr. He was thinking hard. He really liked the sound of the word *Frisbie*. He decided to change the name from Pluto Platter to Frisbie. But he didn't know how to spell the word *Frisbie*, so he spelled it the way it sounds, *Frisbee*. And that's what it's been called ever since!

The Wham-O people thought the Frisbee was a great toy. And so it was. Suddenly, all over the country, people were tossing these pieces of plastic around and catching them. They even had their dogs catching them.

Frisbees were selling fast. They were so popular that people began making up games to play with them, like Frisbee golf and Ultimate. It still is one of the most popular toys ever made.

Chapter Five

A New Sport Is Born

The Frisbee was meant to be a toy that you just throw back and forth as a fun thing to do. In the fall of 1967, a group of students at Columbia High School, in Maplewood, New Jersey, were working on the school newspaper.

As a joke, they announced the formation of a Frisbee team. Having invented the Frisbee team, they then decided to take the joke a little further and see if they could make up a game for the Frisbee team to play.

They experimented a lot and borrowed from several other sports, especially football, soccer, and basketball. And the result was a brand new sport! The sport is now known as Ultimate Frisbee. Despite the original joke, many people now take it seriously. There are Ultimate leagues all over the world.

Now, of course, there are many different styles and shapes of Frisbees, from floppy cloth to rigid plastic. One type of flat, hollow Frisbee can be thrown for almost a quarter of a mile!

About Ultimate

Ultimate is played in teams on a field like a football field. The players toss the Frisbee to members of their own team while the players on other team try to intercept it. When a player drops a Frisbee, the other team gets to throw it. To score, you have to catch a Frisbee inside the opposing team's goal area.

Back then, Joel Silver, one of the students responsible for that student newspaper prank, had said, "Someday people all over the world will be playing this game."

The other students laughed and said, "Yeah, Joel, sure!"

But he was right. More than thirty years have passed, and now Ultimate is played in forty-two countries. More than 50,000 people play this game in the United States, and the number is growing all the time.